Beautiful Butterflies

A GRAYSCALE ADULT COLORING BOOK

Unique and enchanting pages of these delicate creatures for you to bring to life.

Watch as your imagination takes flight,
with each butterfly growing more picturesque
with every turn of a page.

I0482457

Beautiful Butterflies is a remarkable way to unwind,
relax and just be.

These grayscale images are designed to stimulate your
creativity, improve your fine motor skills, and induce a
state of calm meditative focus.

Fine tip markers, colored pencils and watercolor
mediums are all ideal for bringing these pages to life.

COLORING IN GRAYSCALE: THE BASICS

COLORS

The existing shading on grayscale pages creates a beautiful, rich color palette when blended with multiple shades of the same color. Using multiple variations of blue, green, yellow, etc. will allow you to create a more lifelike final image.

MATERIALS

Colored pencils, watercolor pencils, blendable markers and crayons all work well for grayscale coloring. Use gel pens, fine tipped markers to enhance detail, and a watercolor brush or sponge for better blending technique.

BLENDING WITH GRAYSCALE

Try coloring over the darker gray areas with your darkest color shades for greater depth and saturation.

HAVE FUN

There is no wrong way to color. Just do what feels right!

CONNECT WITH US

We love seeing all the gorgeous works of art created with our grayscale coloring books. Post photos of your finished pages with your Amazon review, tweet at @HartGrayscale, or share them in the Grayscale Coloring Group on Facebook!

Materials Used:

Colored By:

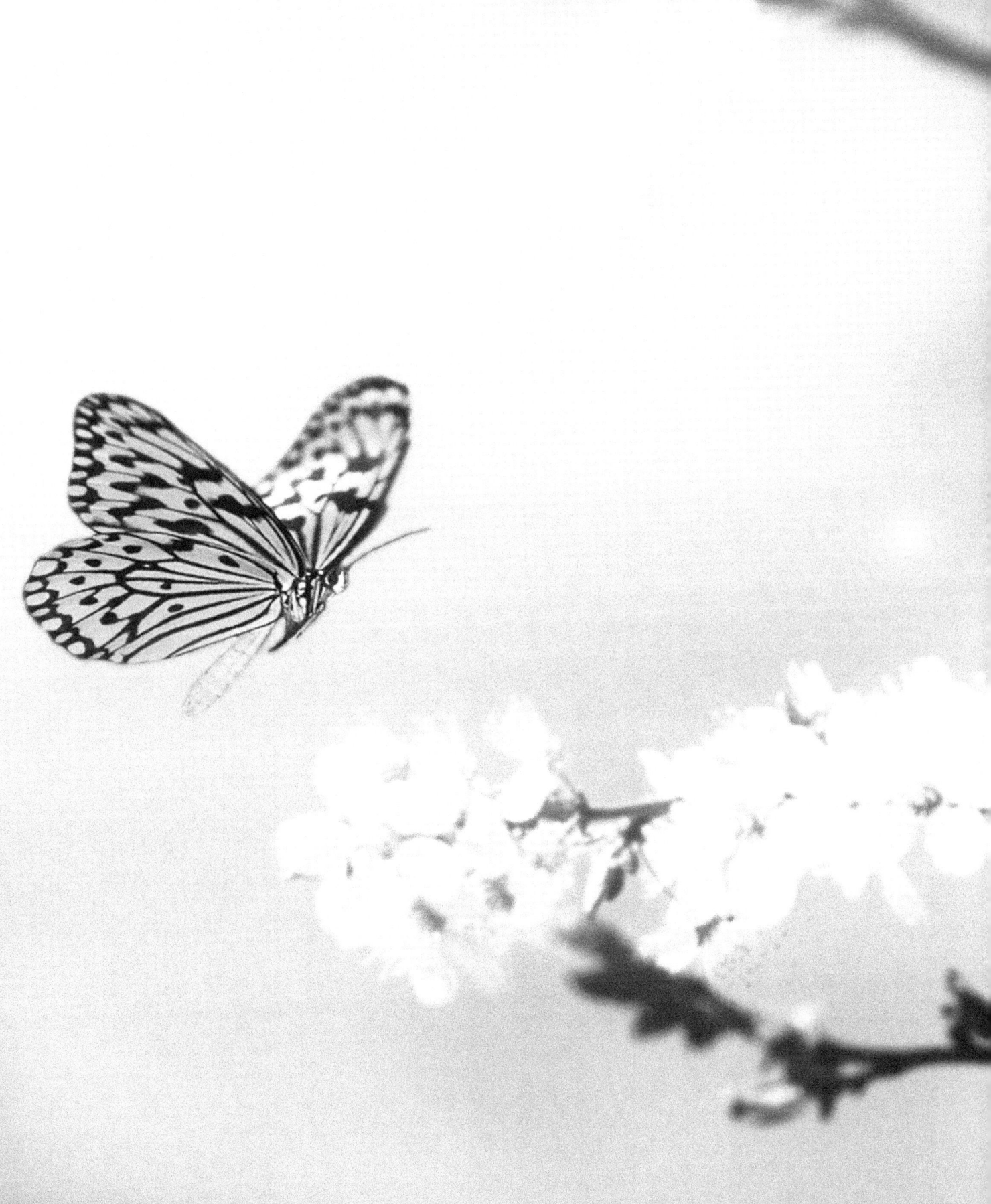

Materials Used:

Colored By:

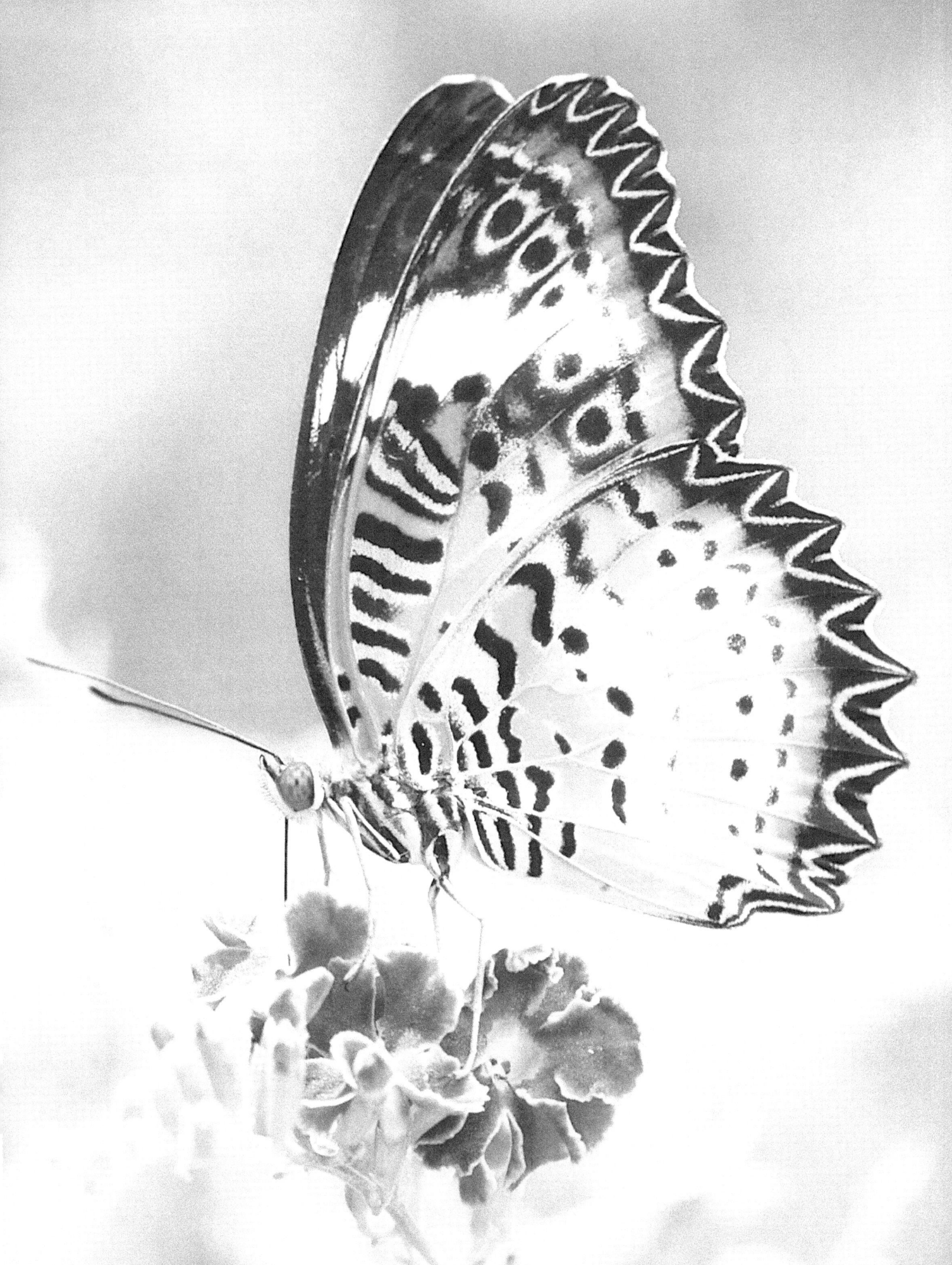

Materials Used:

Colored By:

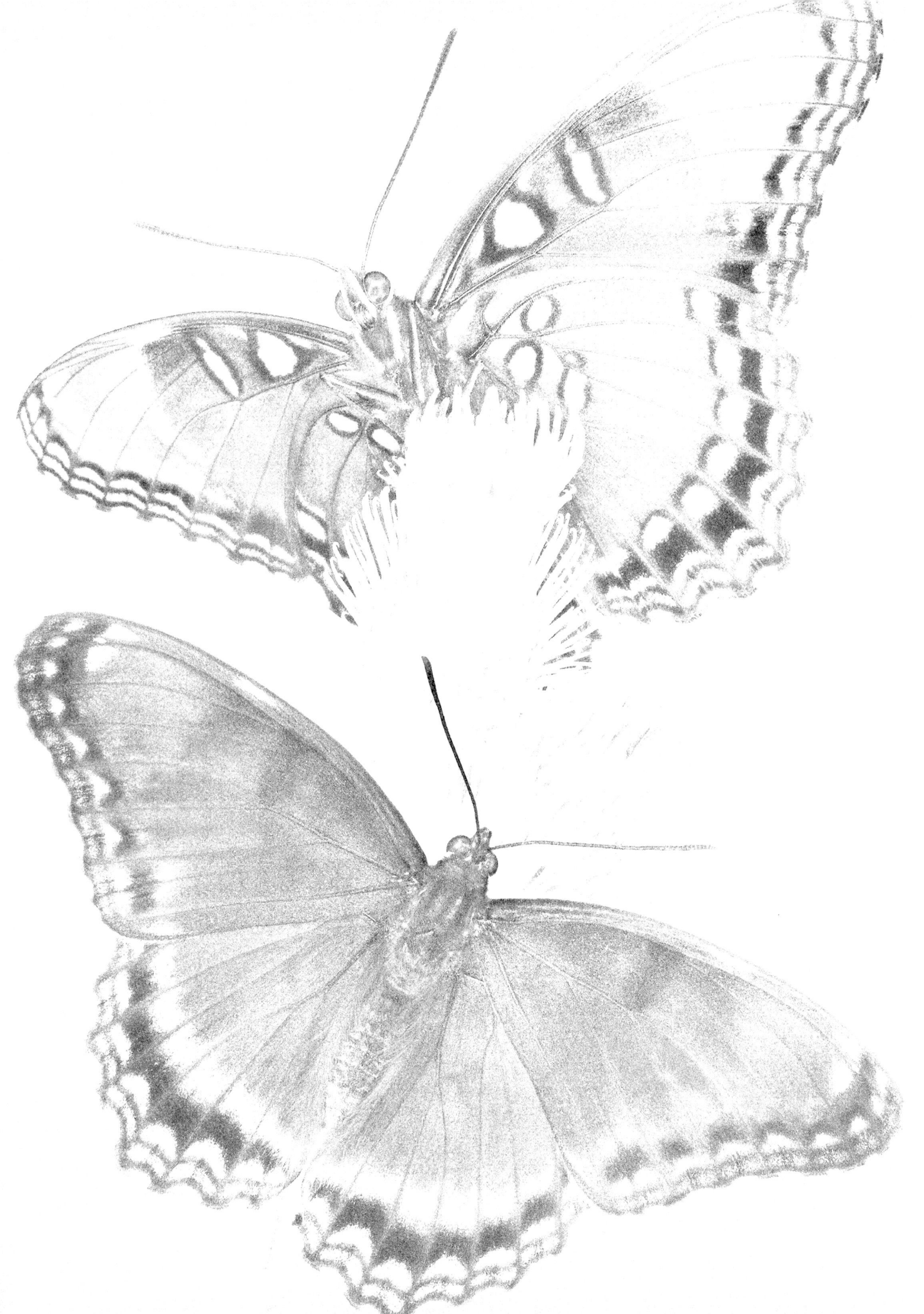

Materials Used:

Colored By:

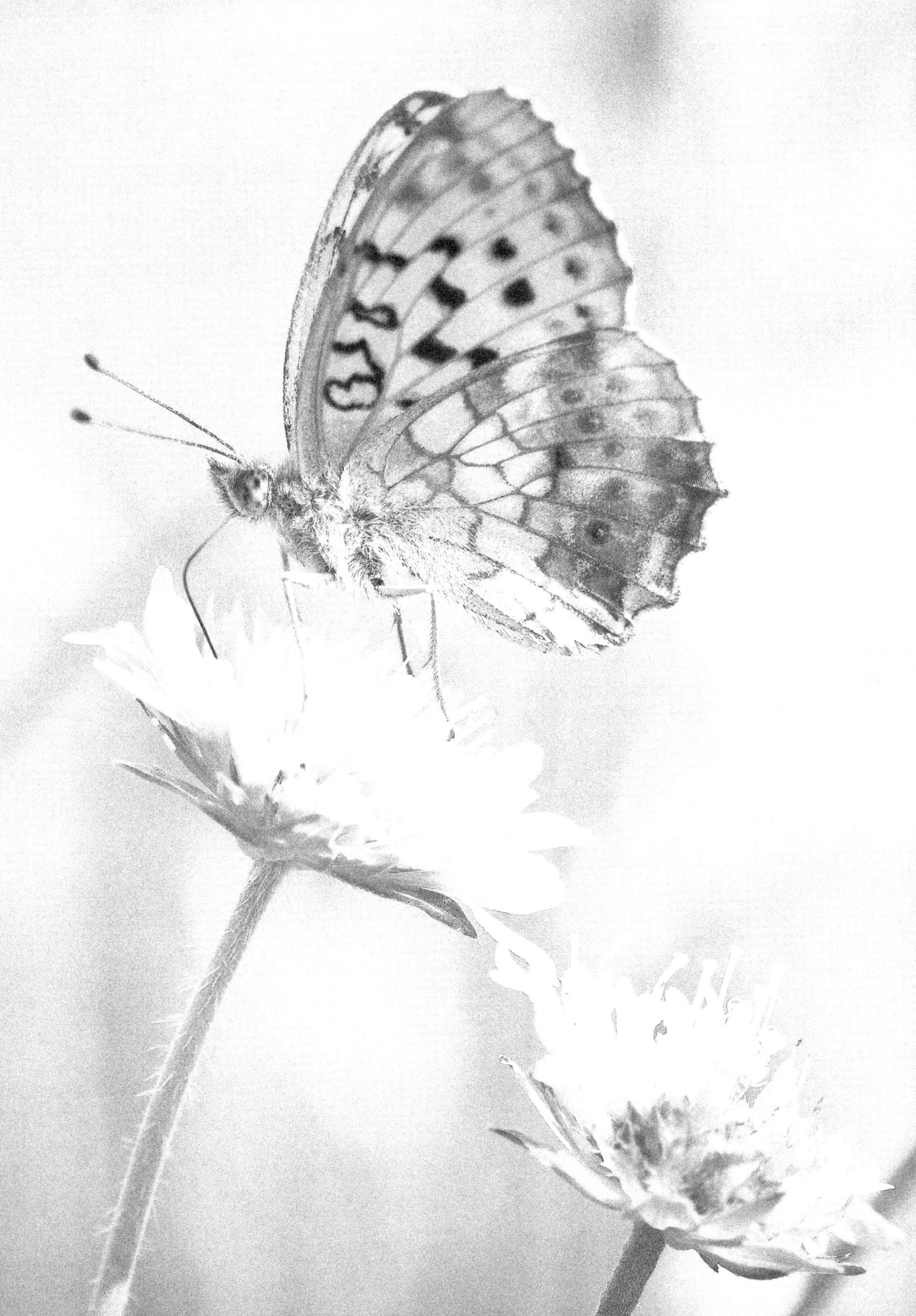

Materials Used:

Colored By:

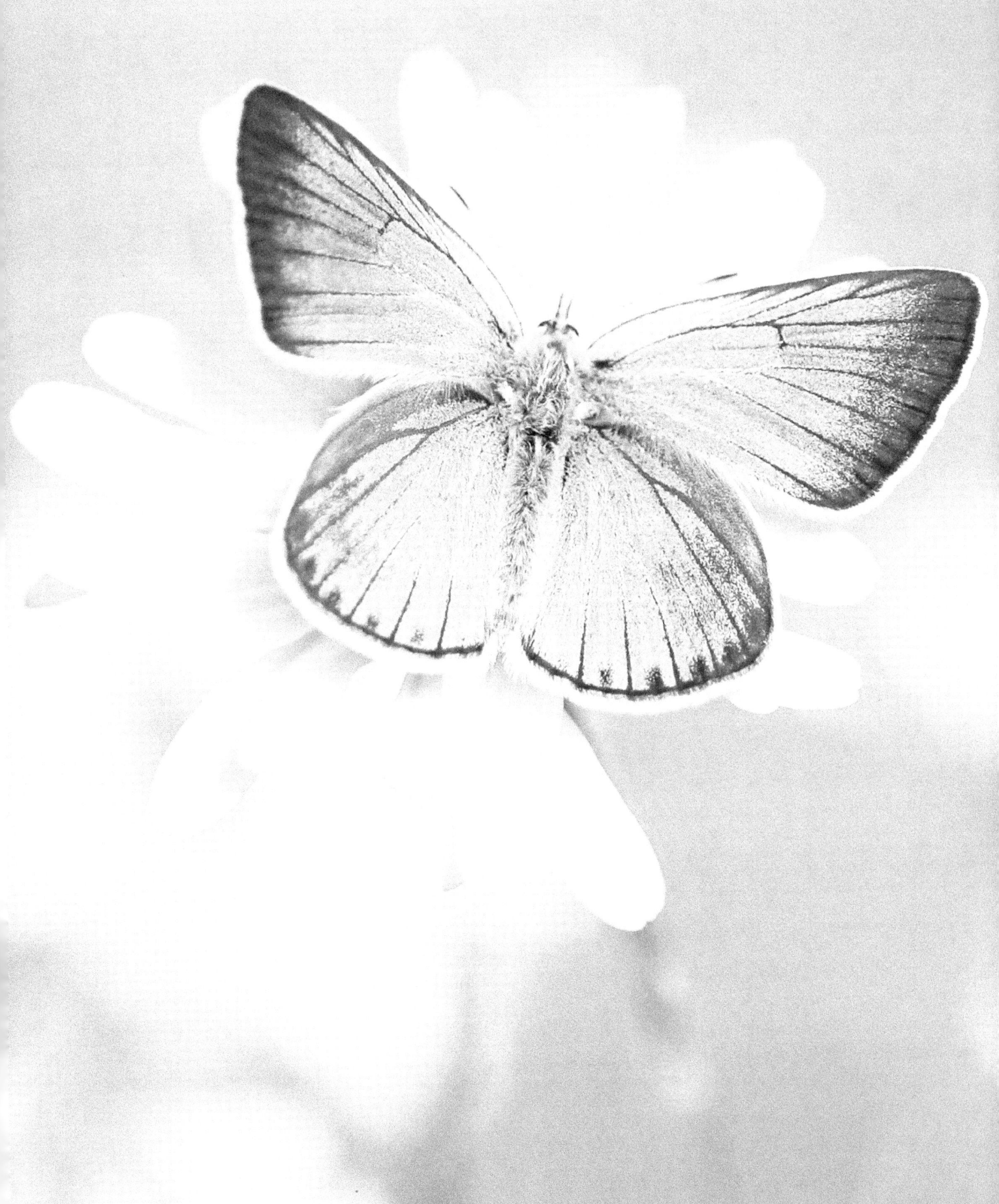

Materials Used:

Colored By:

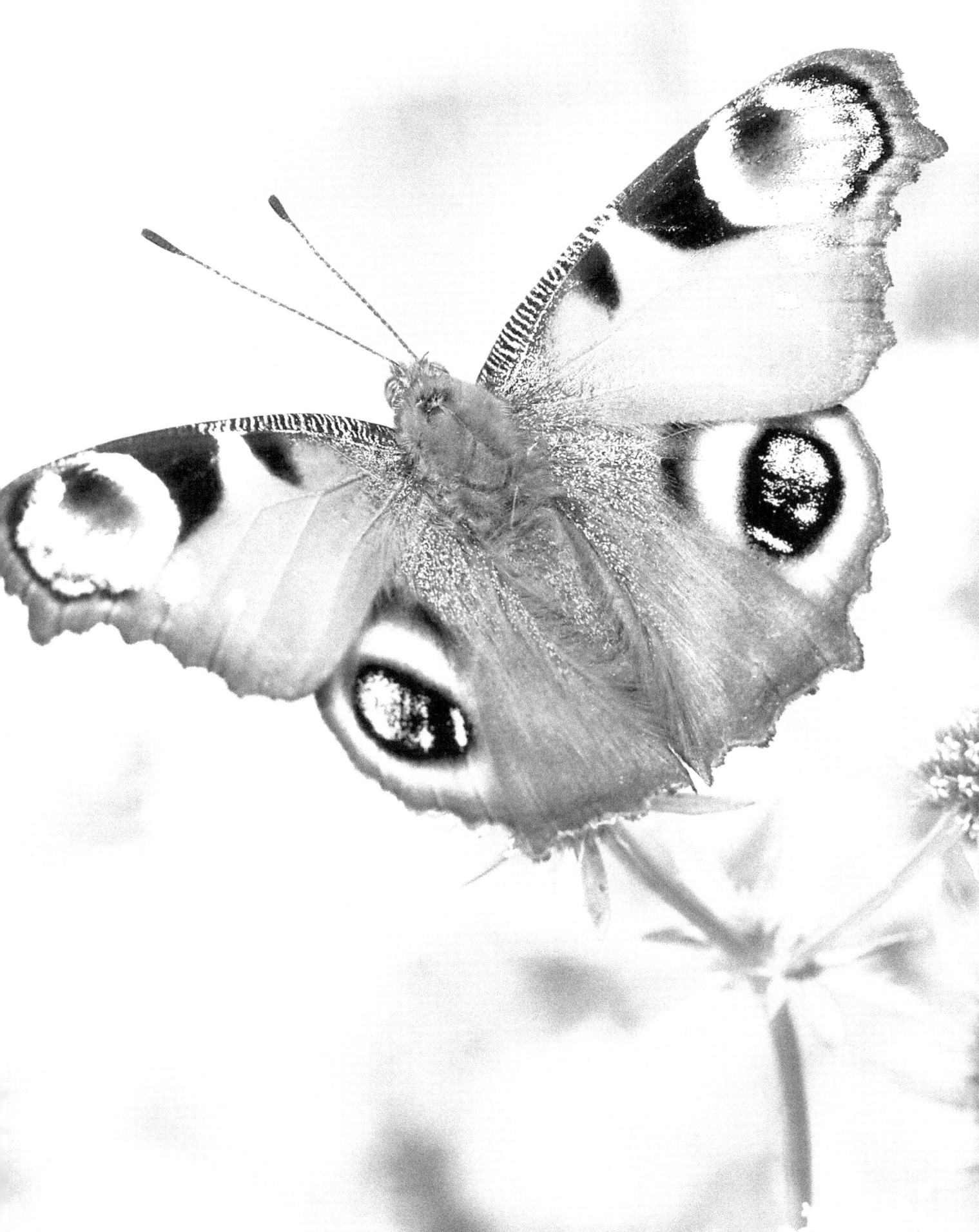

Materials Used:

Colored By:

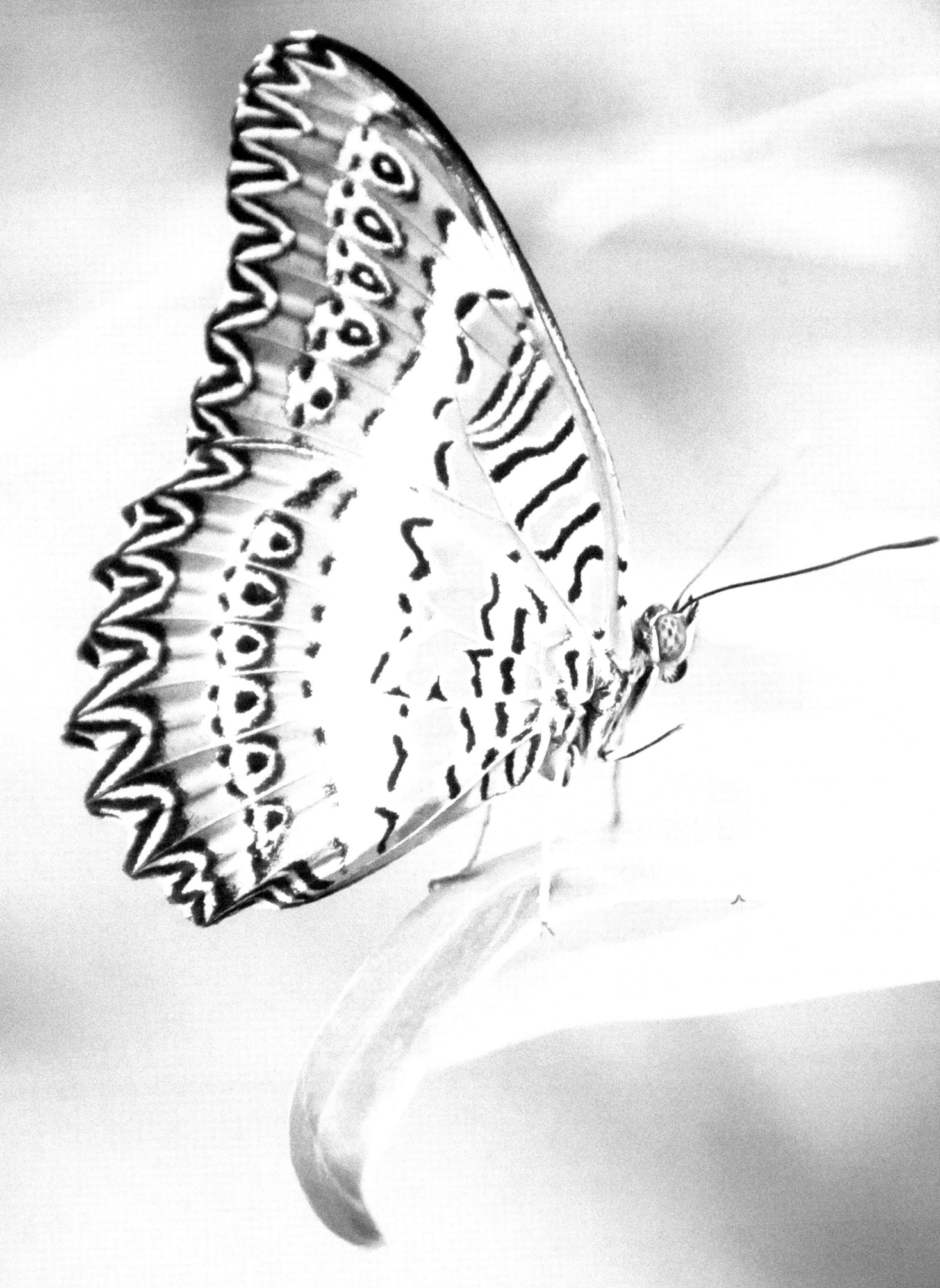

Materials Used:

Colored By:

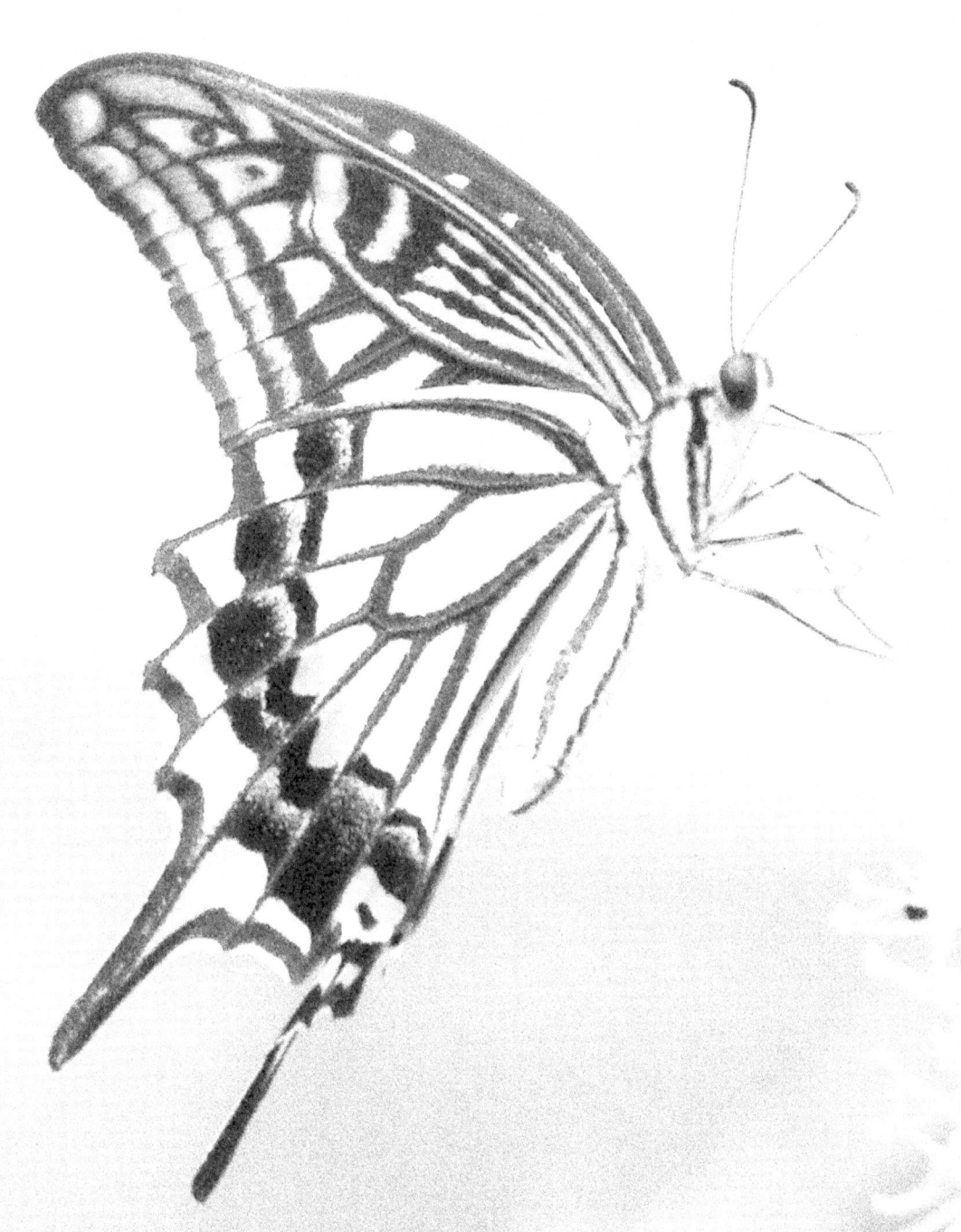

Materials Used:

Colored By:

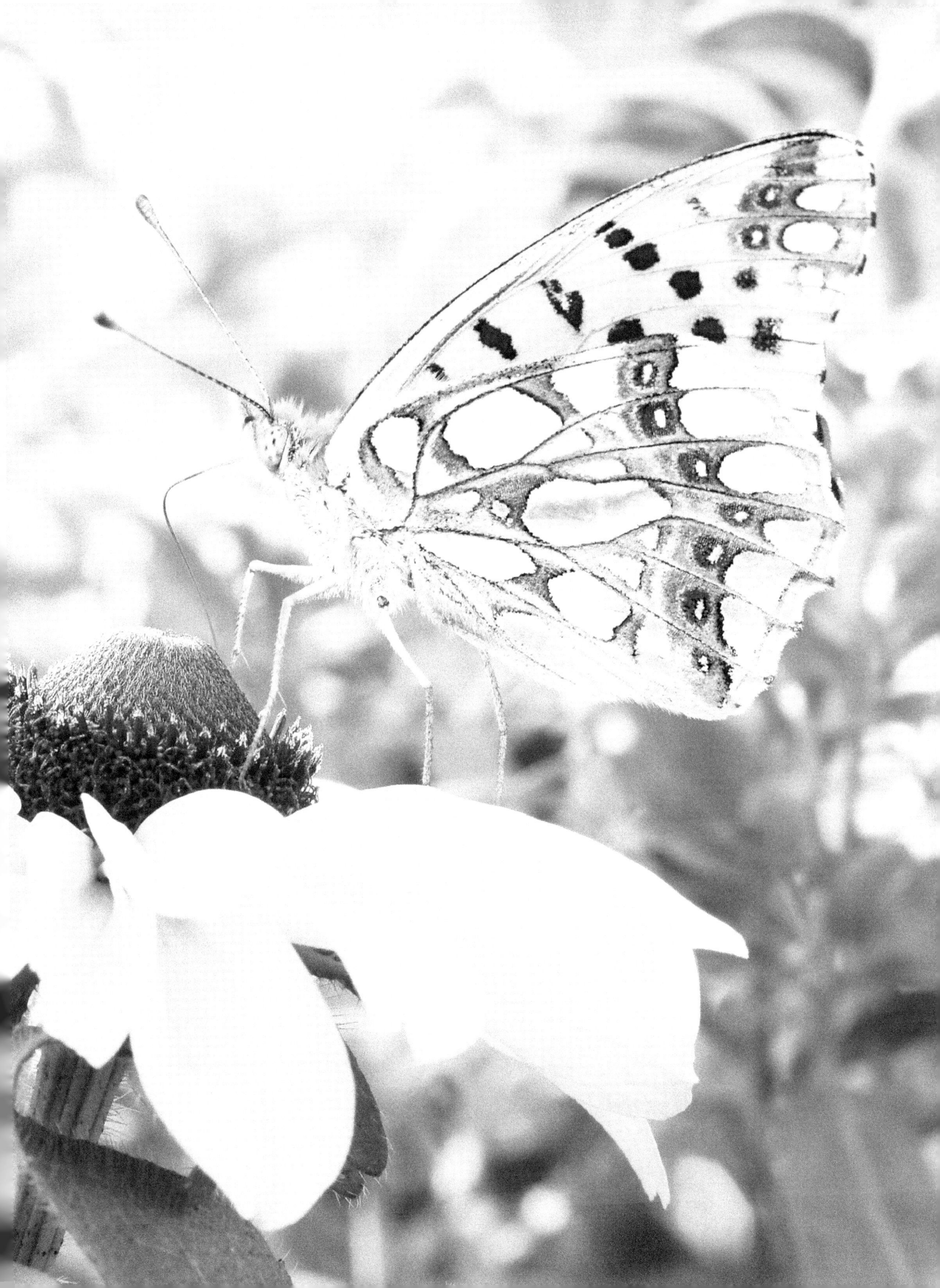

Materials Used:

Colored By:

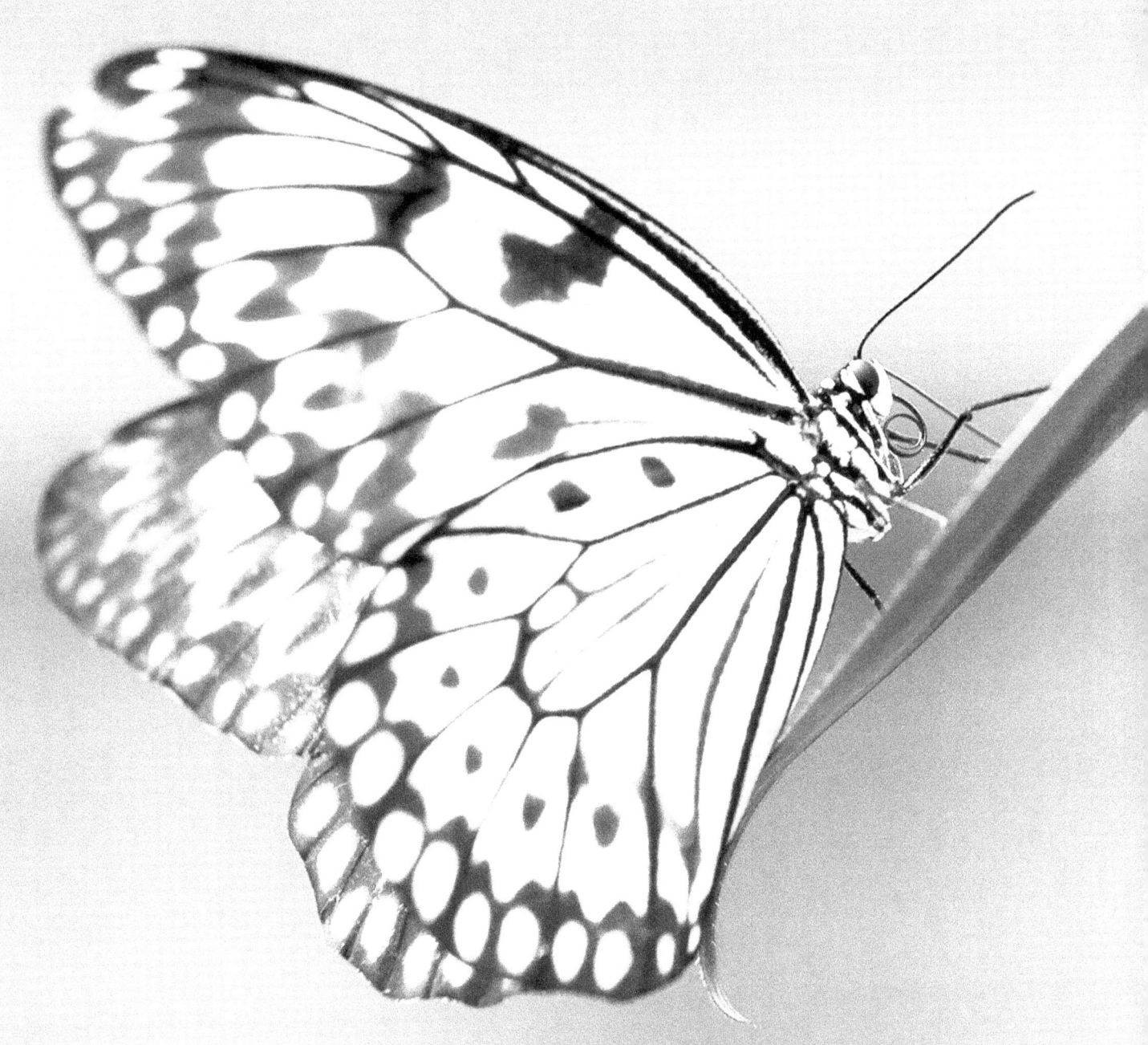

Materials Used:

Colored By:

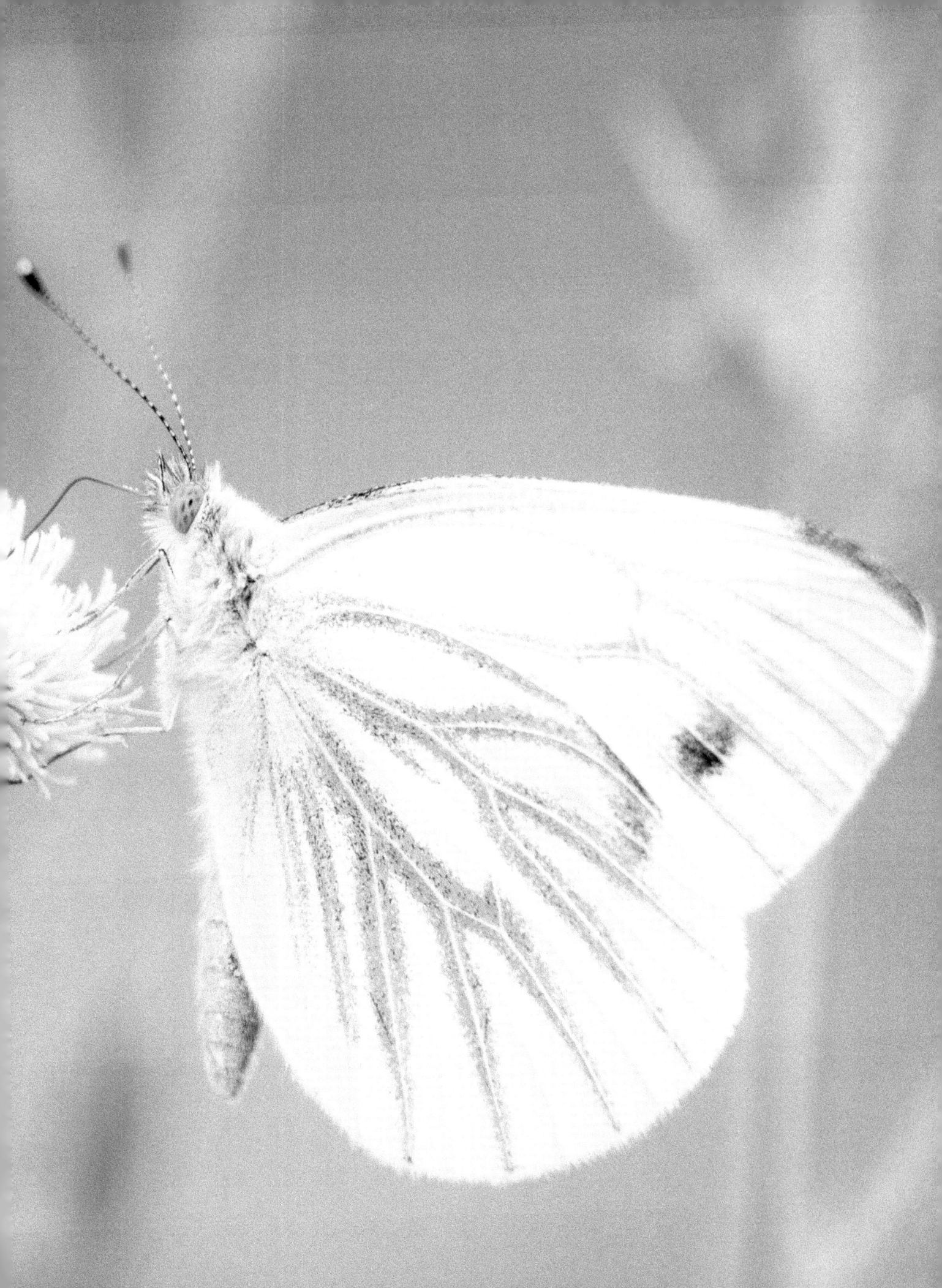

Materials Used:

Colored By:

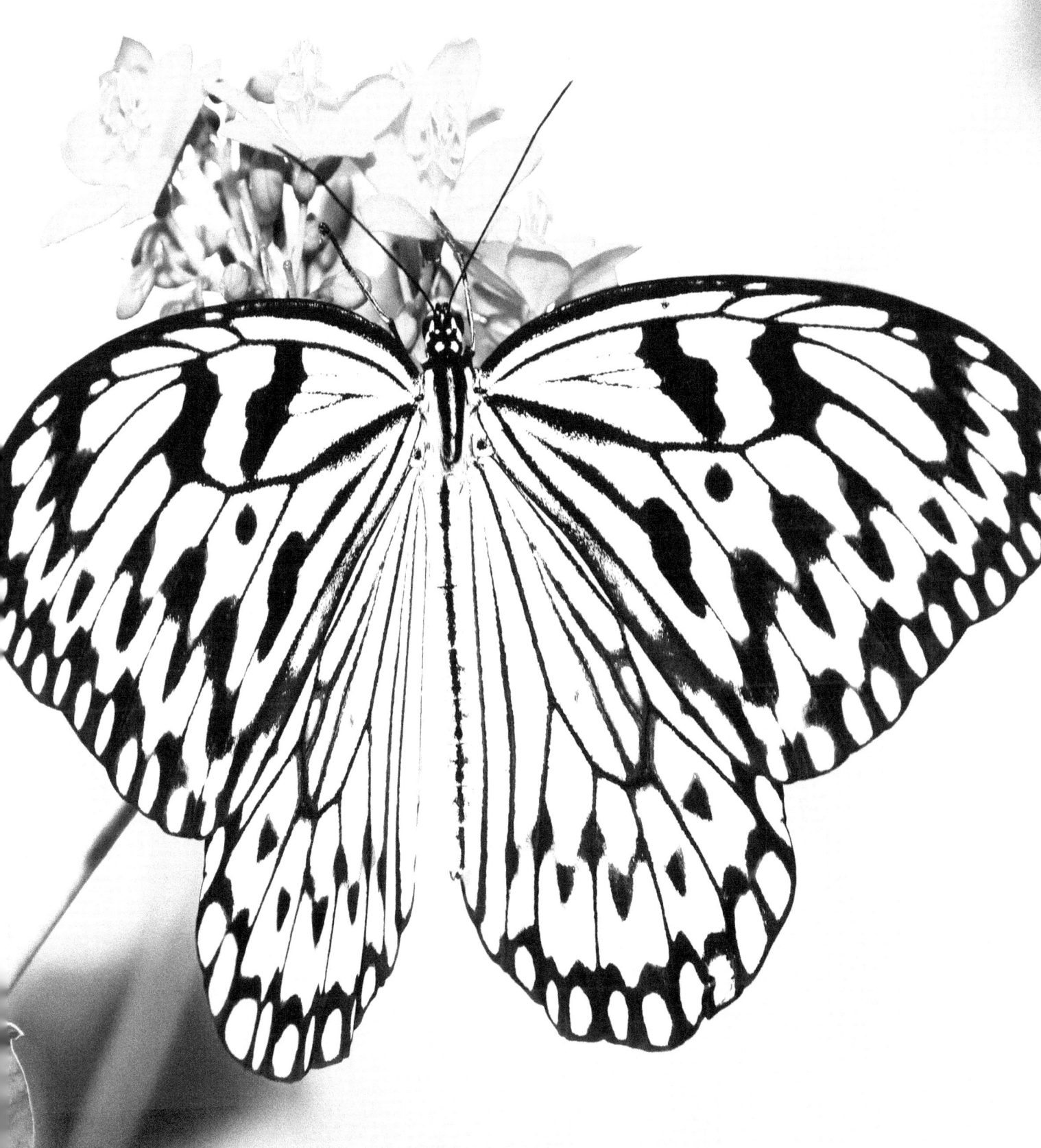

Materials Used:

Colored By:

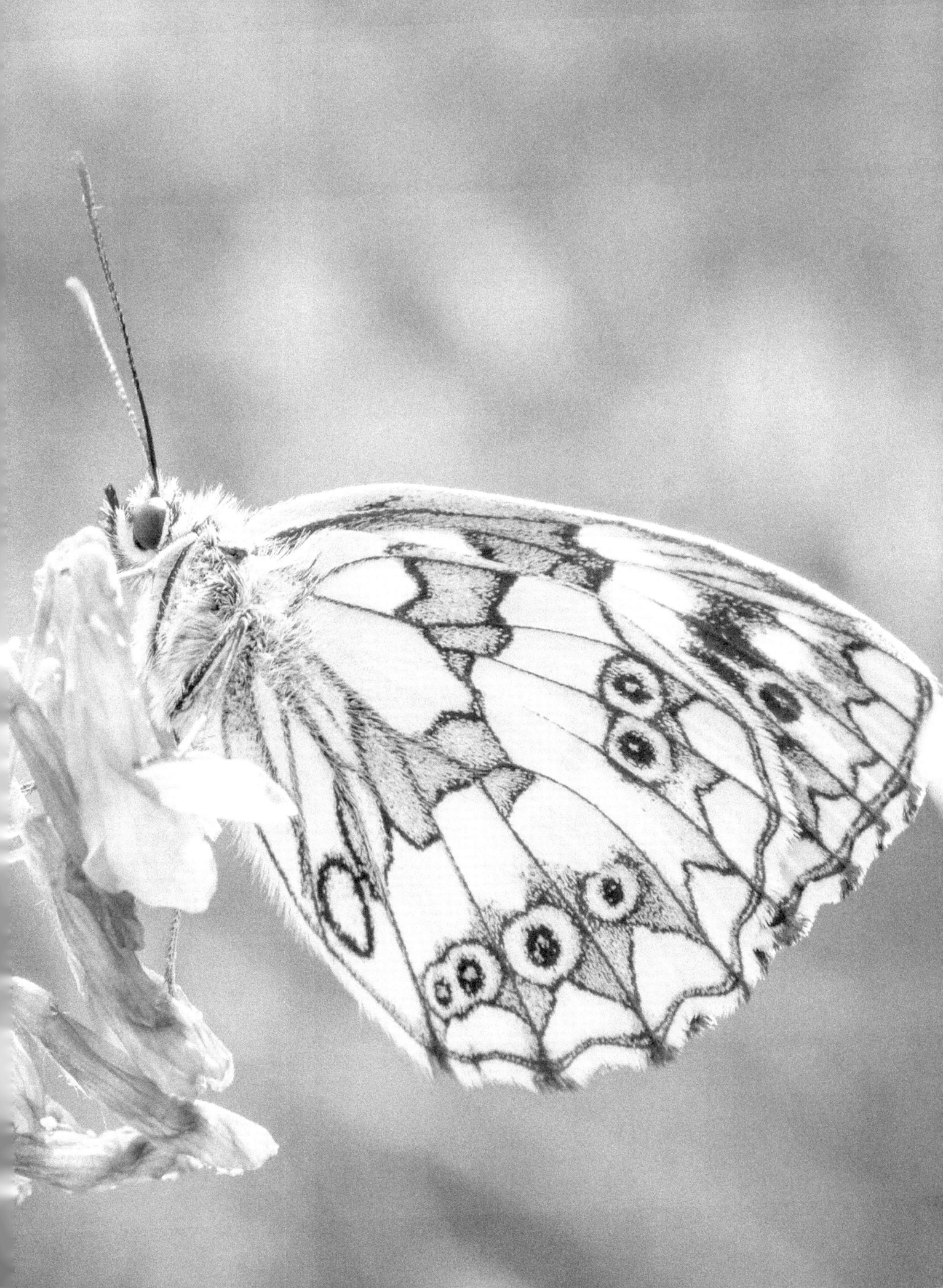

Materials Used:

Colored By:

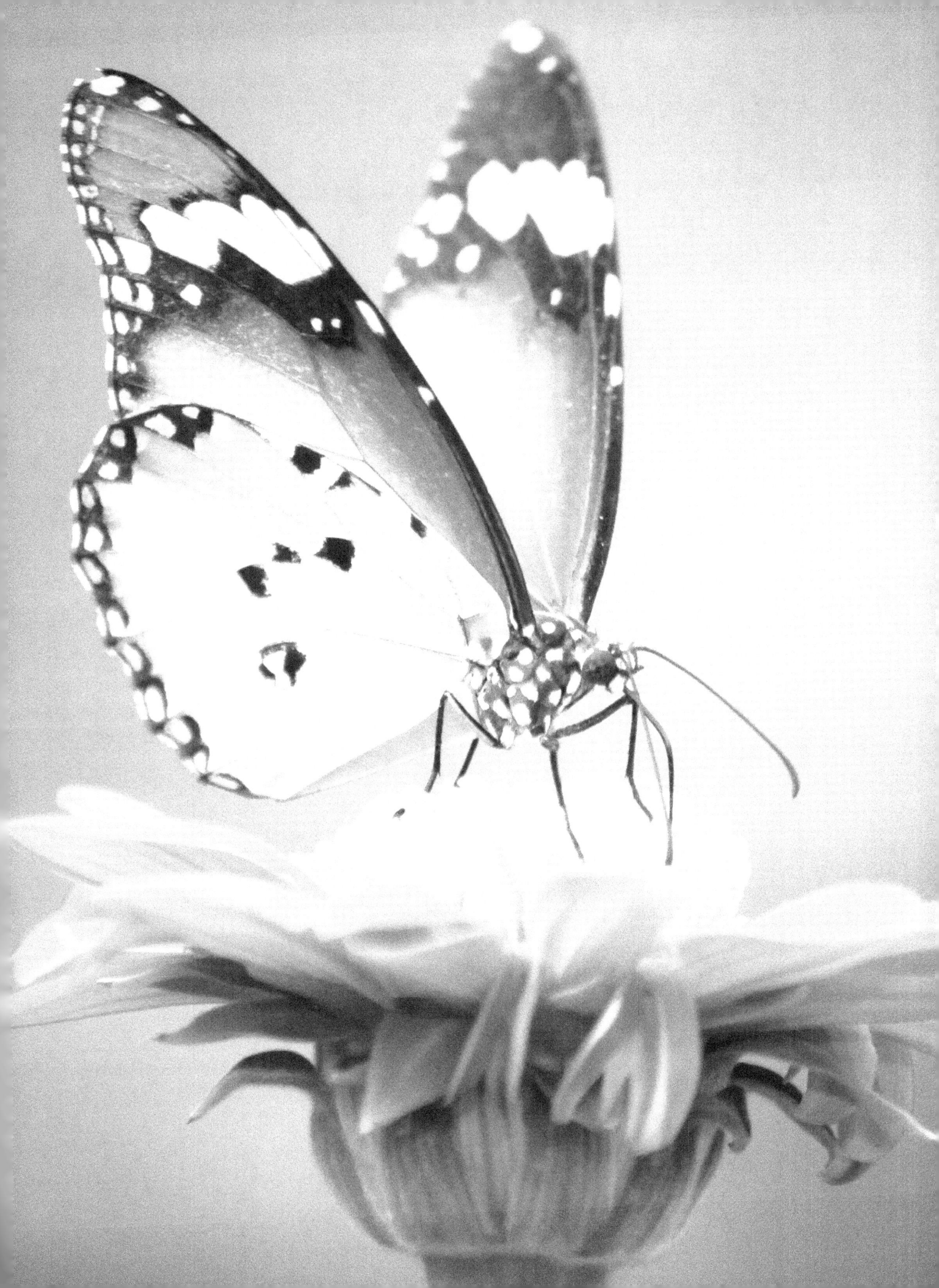

Materials Used:

Colored By:

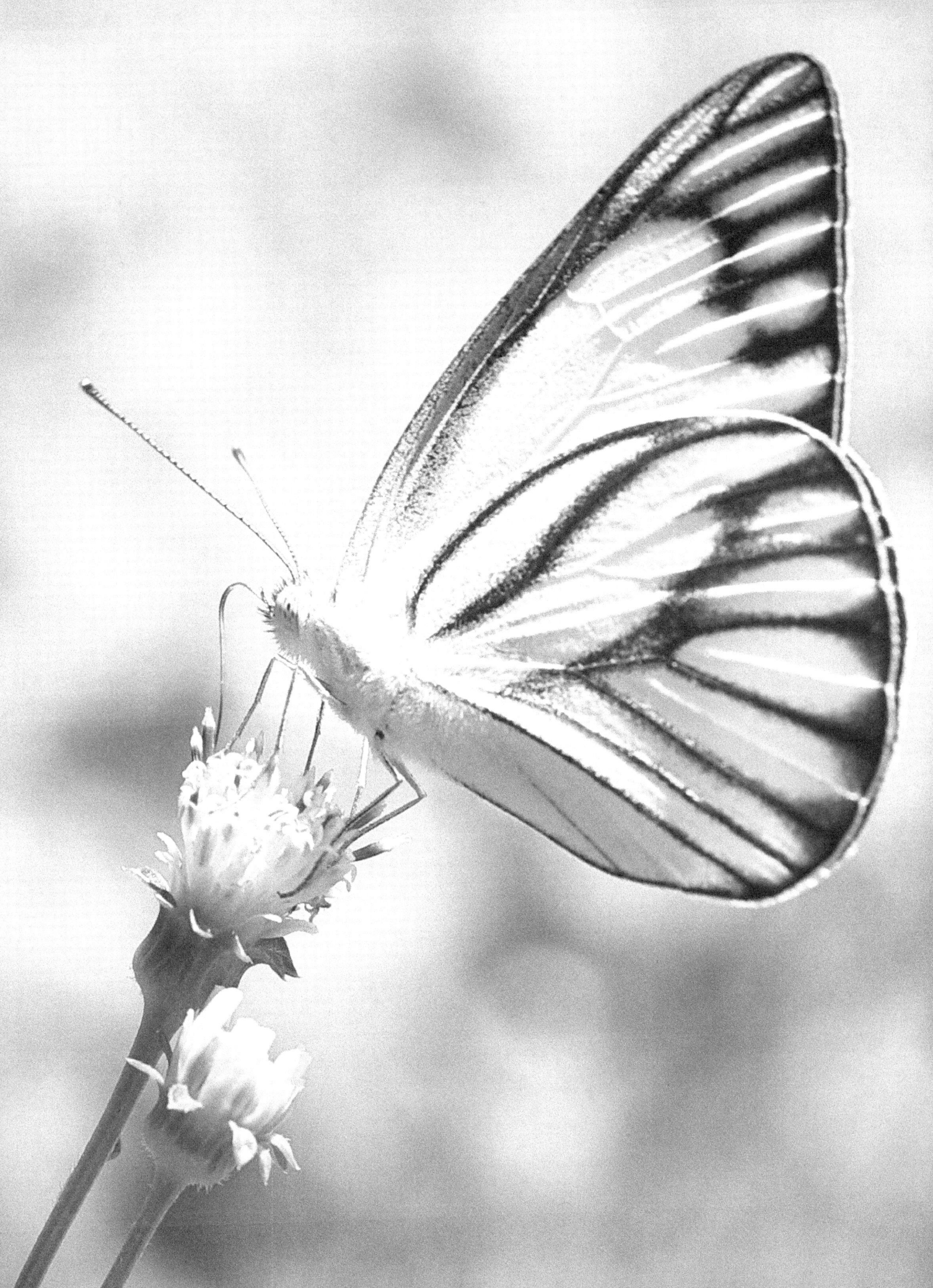

Materials Used:

Colored By:

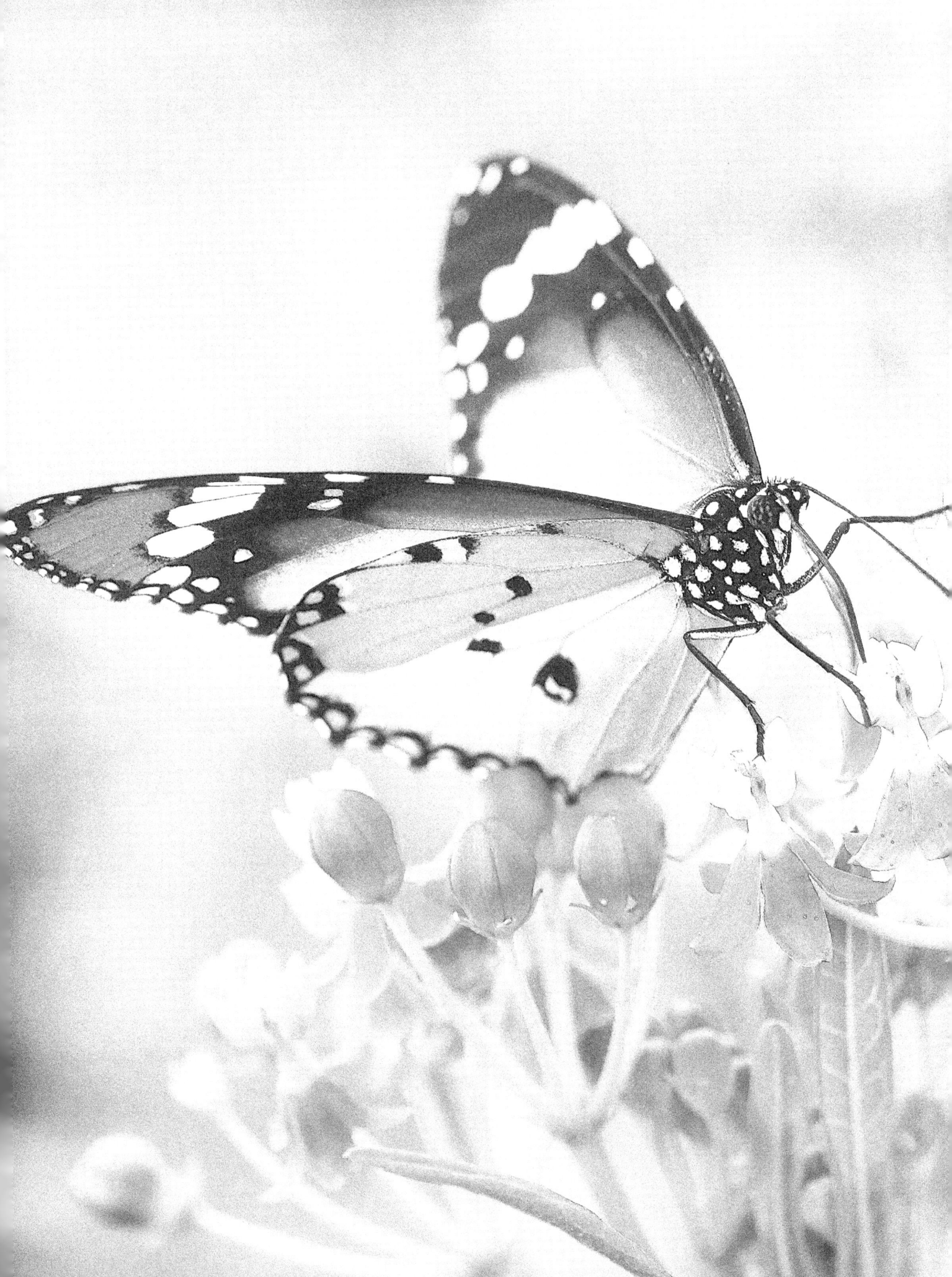

Materials Used:

Colored By:

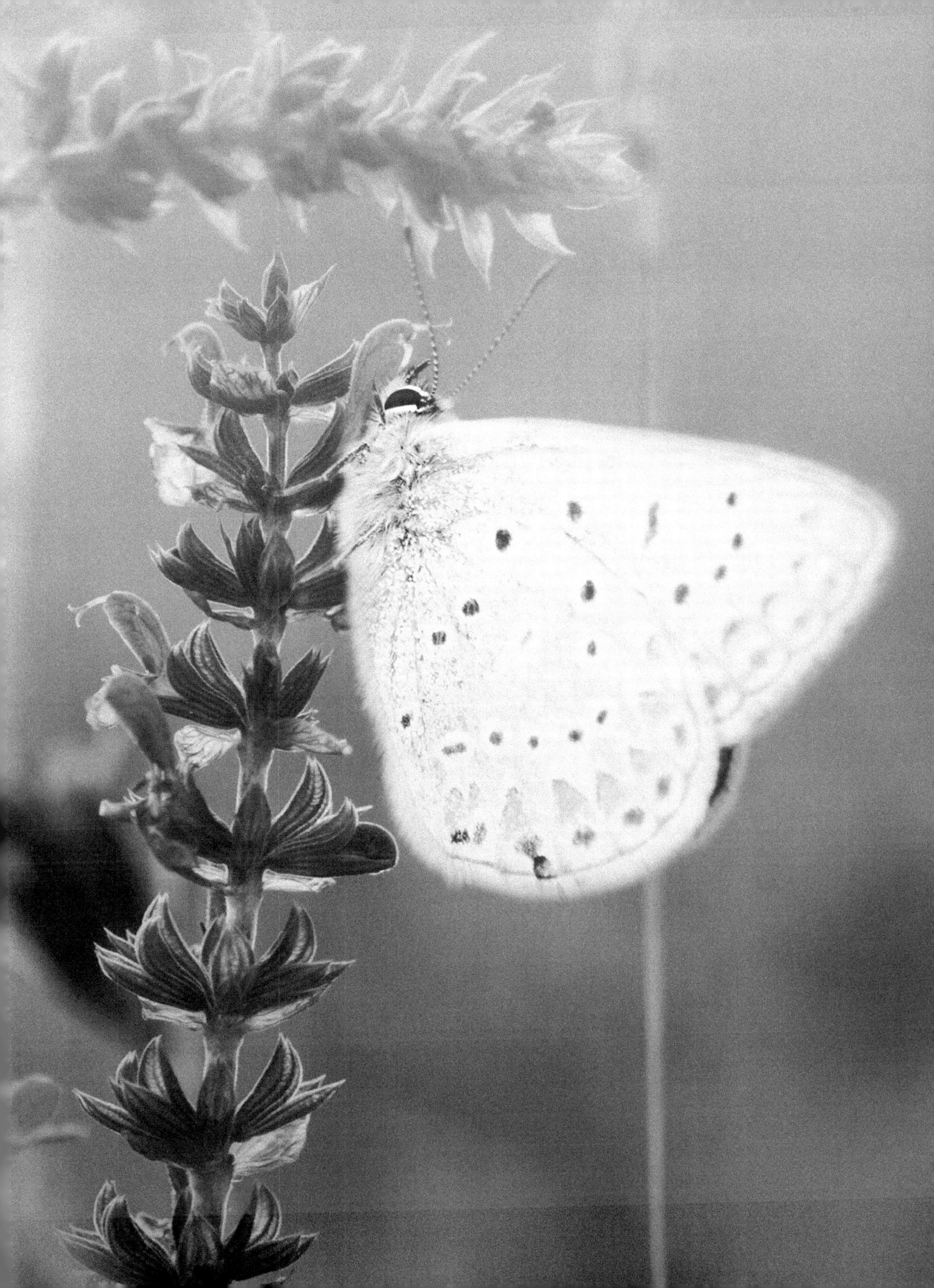

Materials Used:

Colored By:

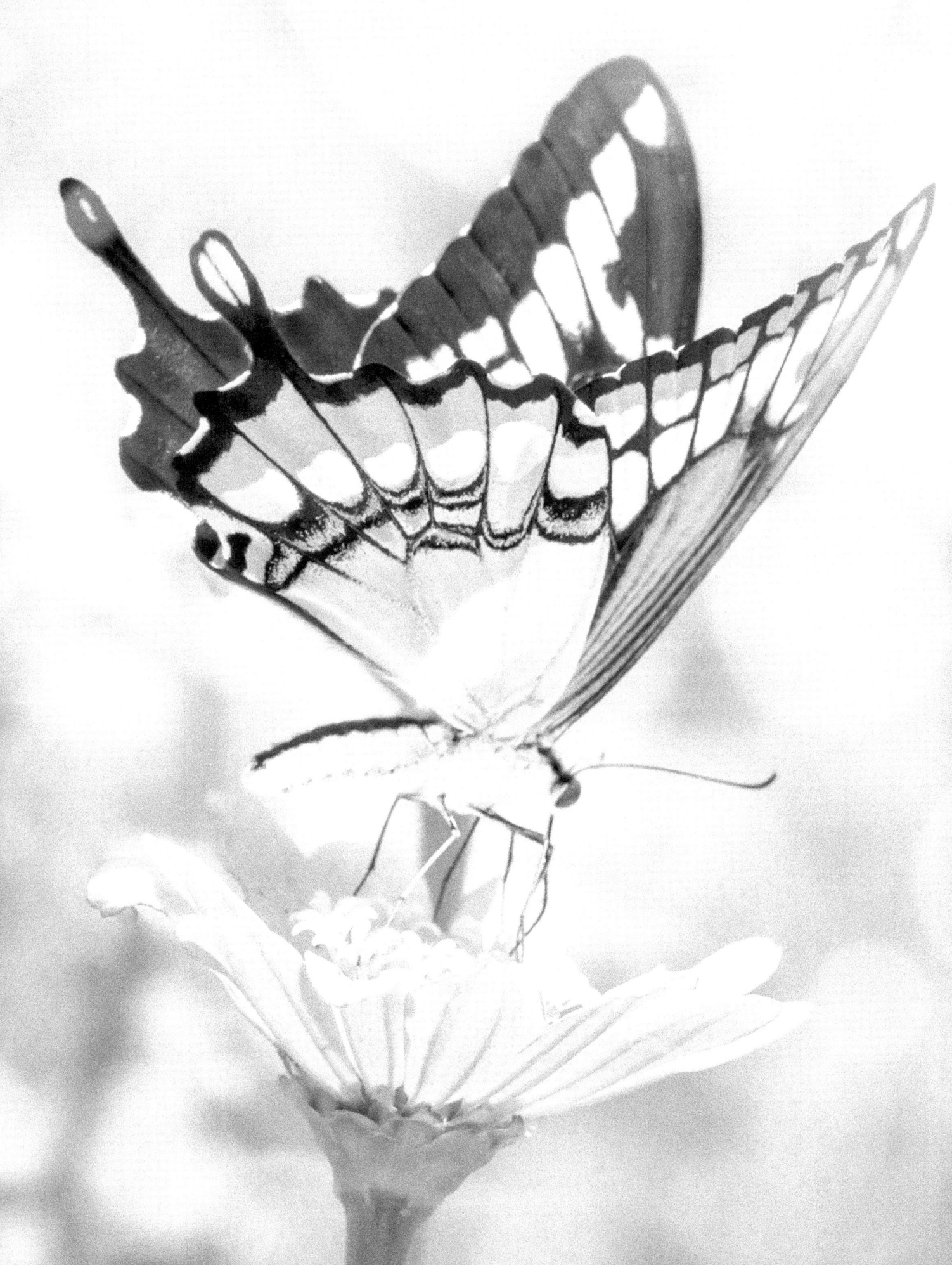

Materials Used:

Colored By:

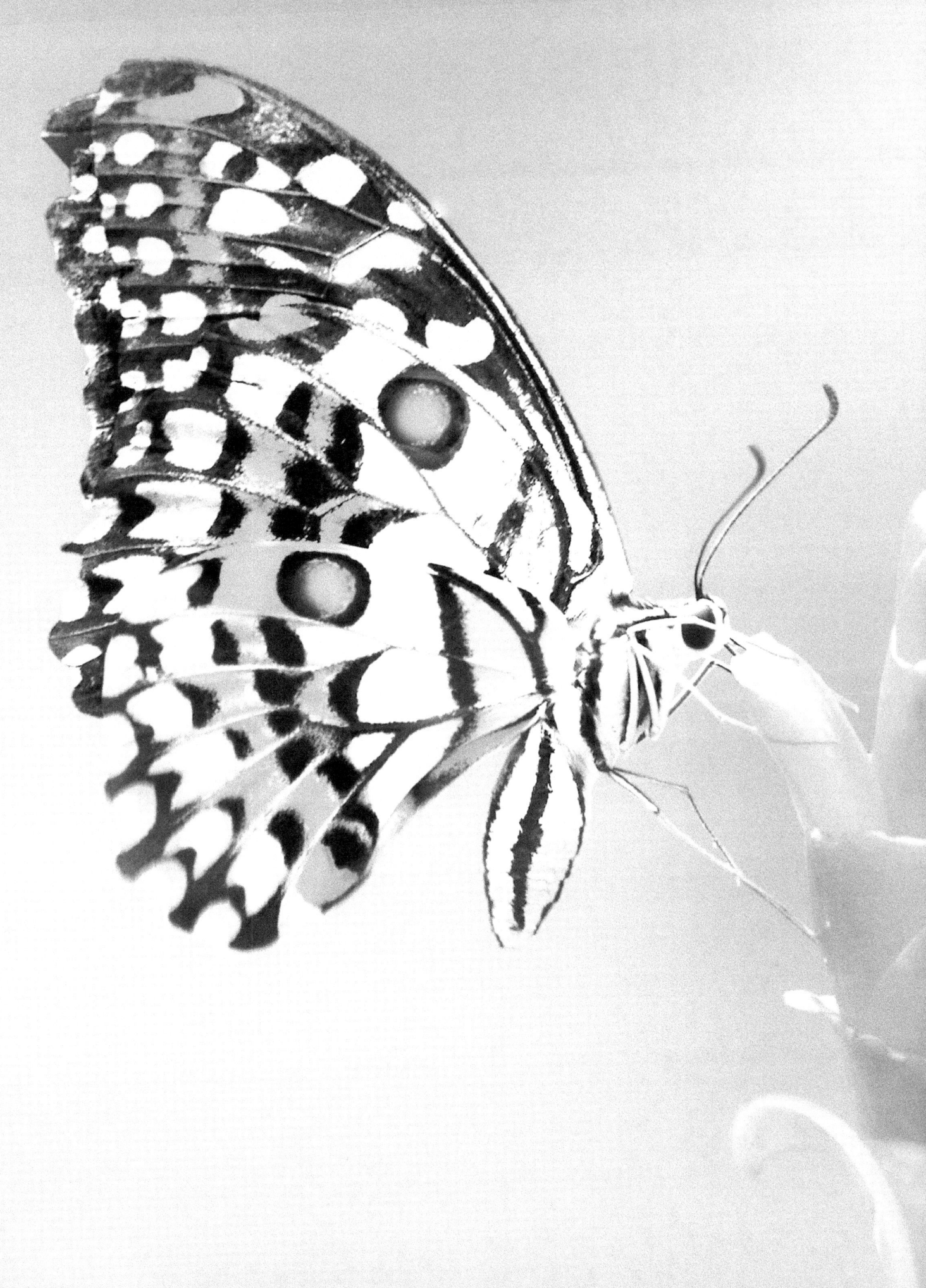

Materials Used:

Colored By:

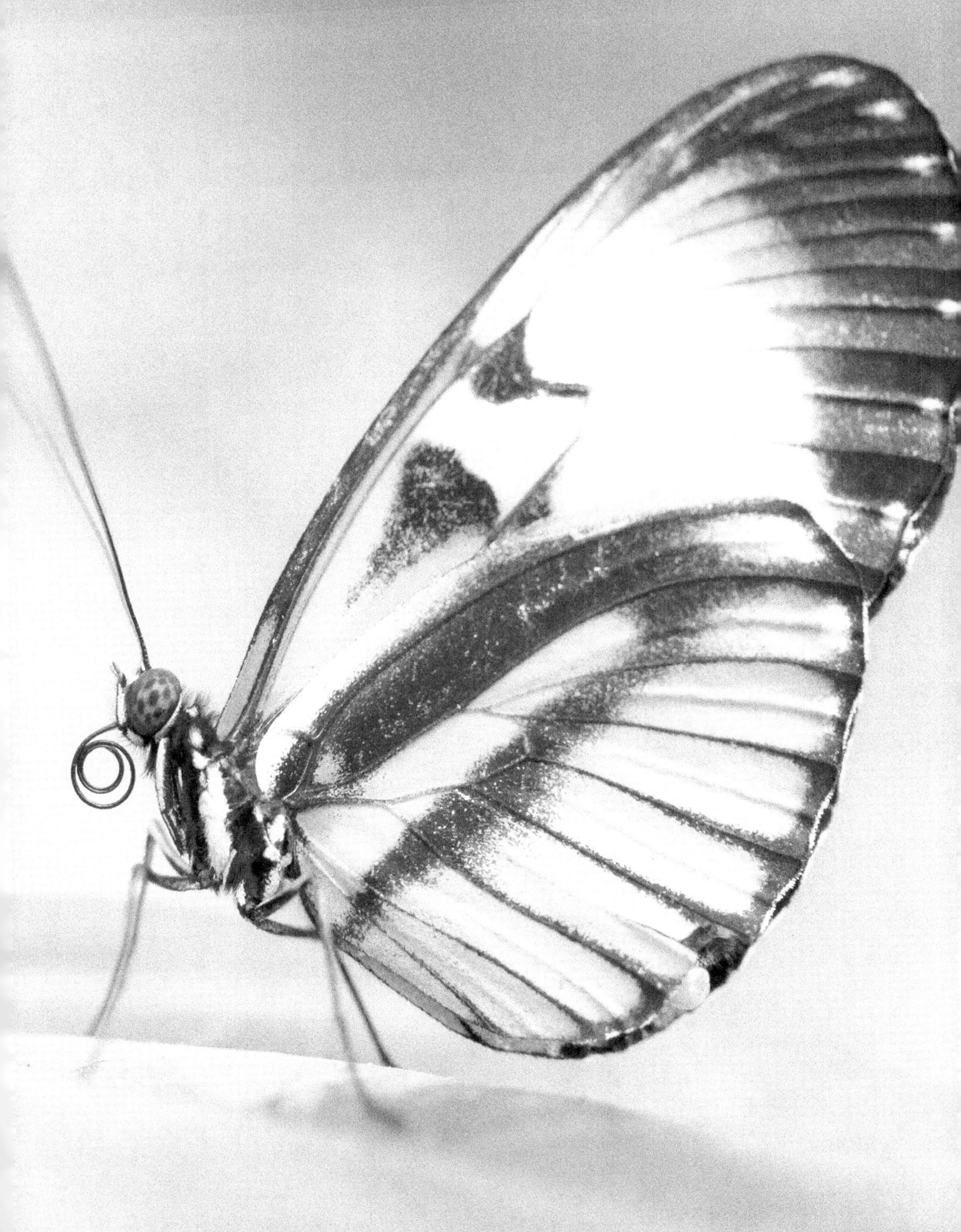

Materials Used:

Colored By:

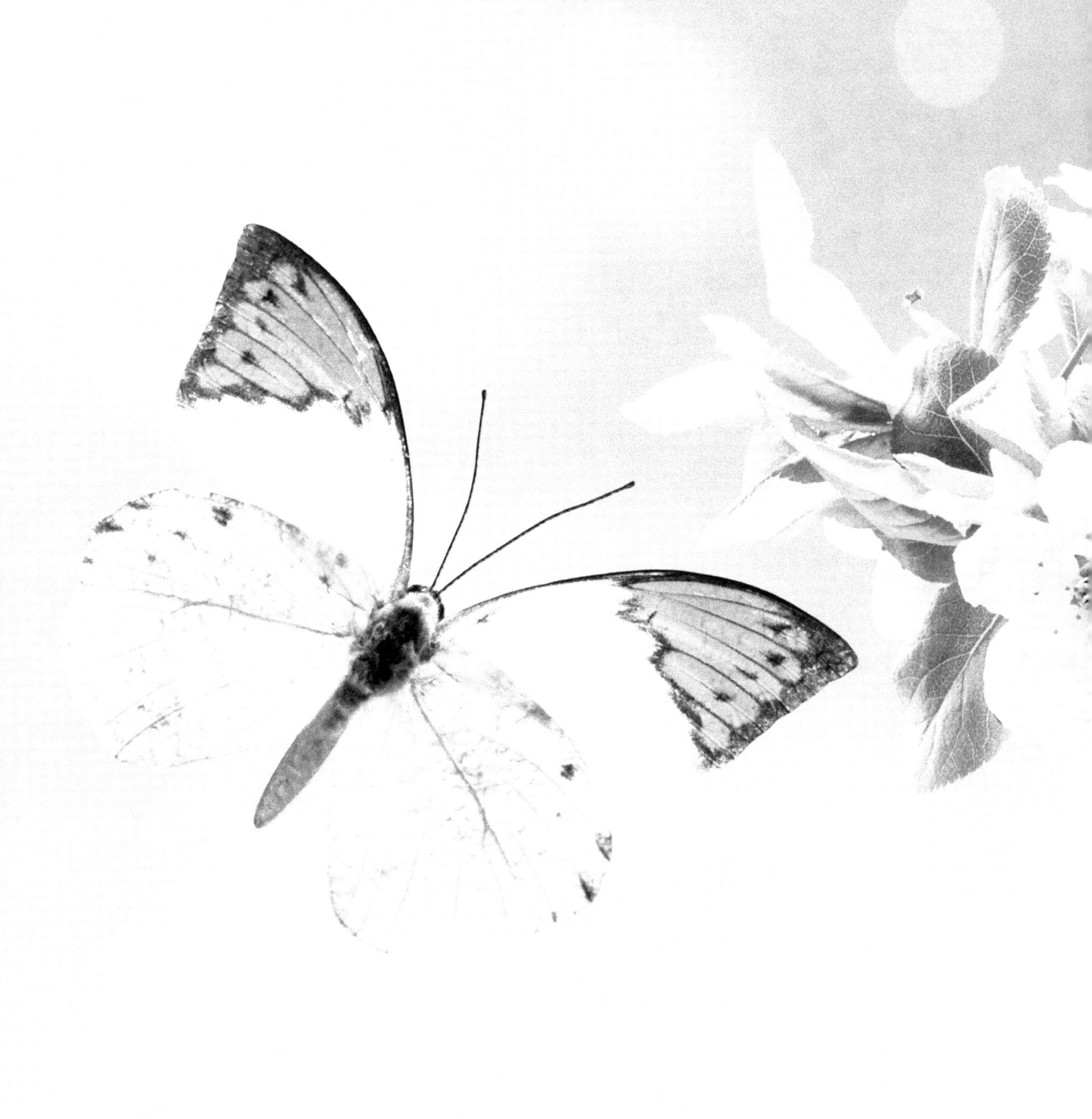

Materials Used:

Colored By:

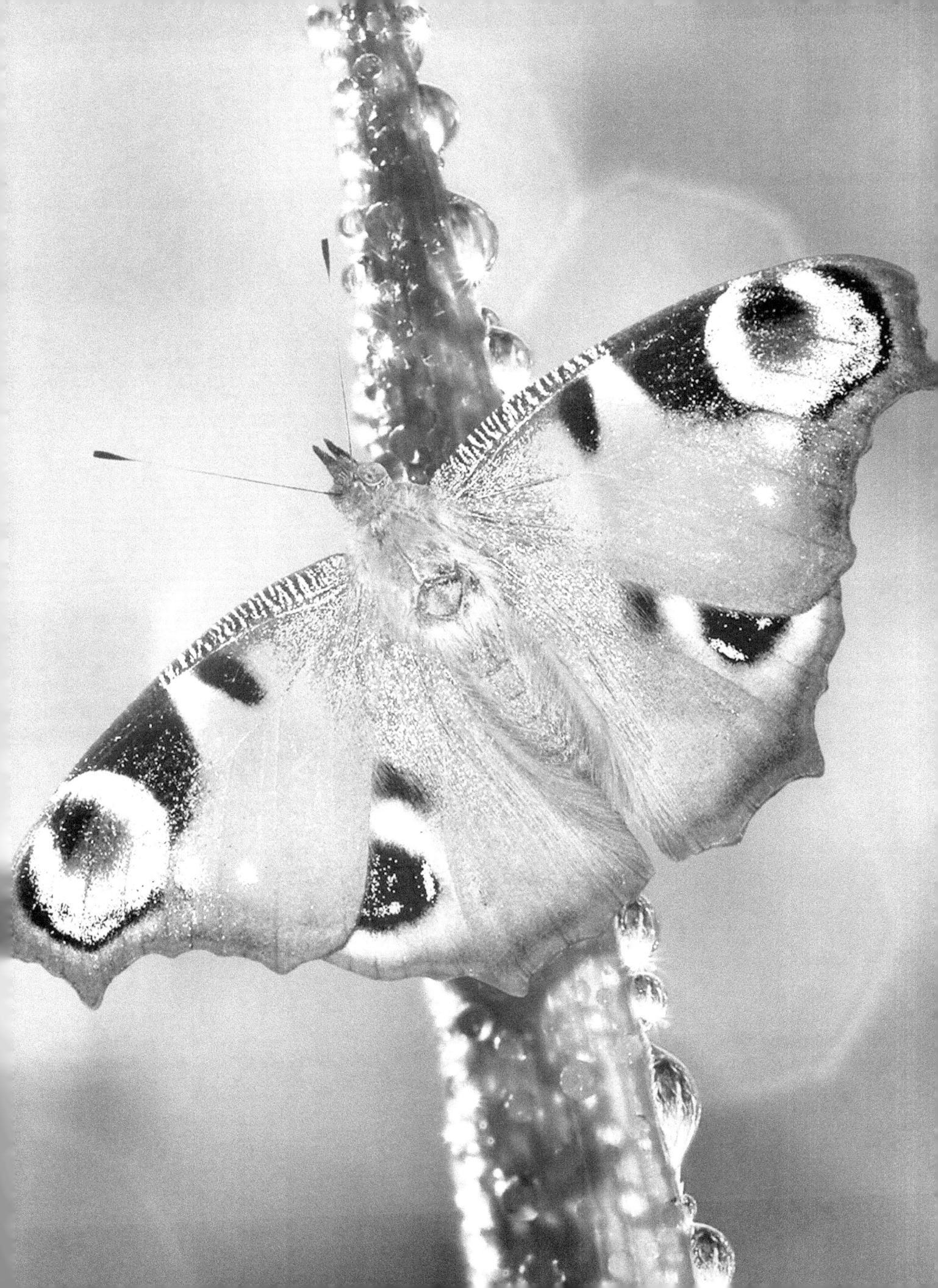

Materials Used:

Colored By:

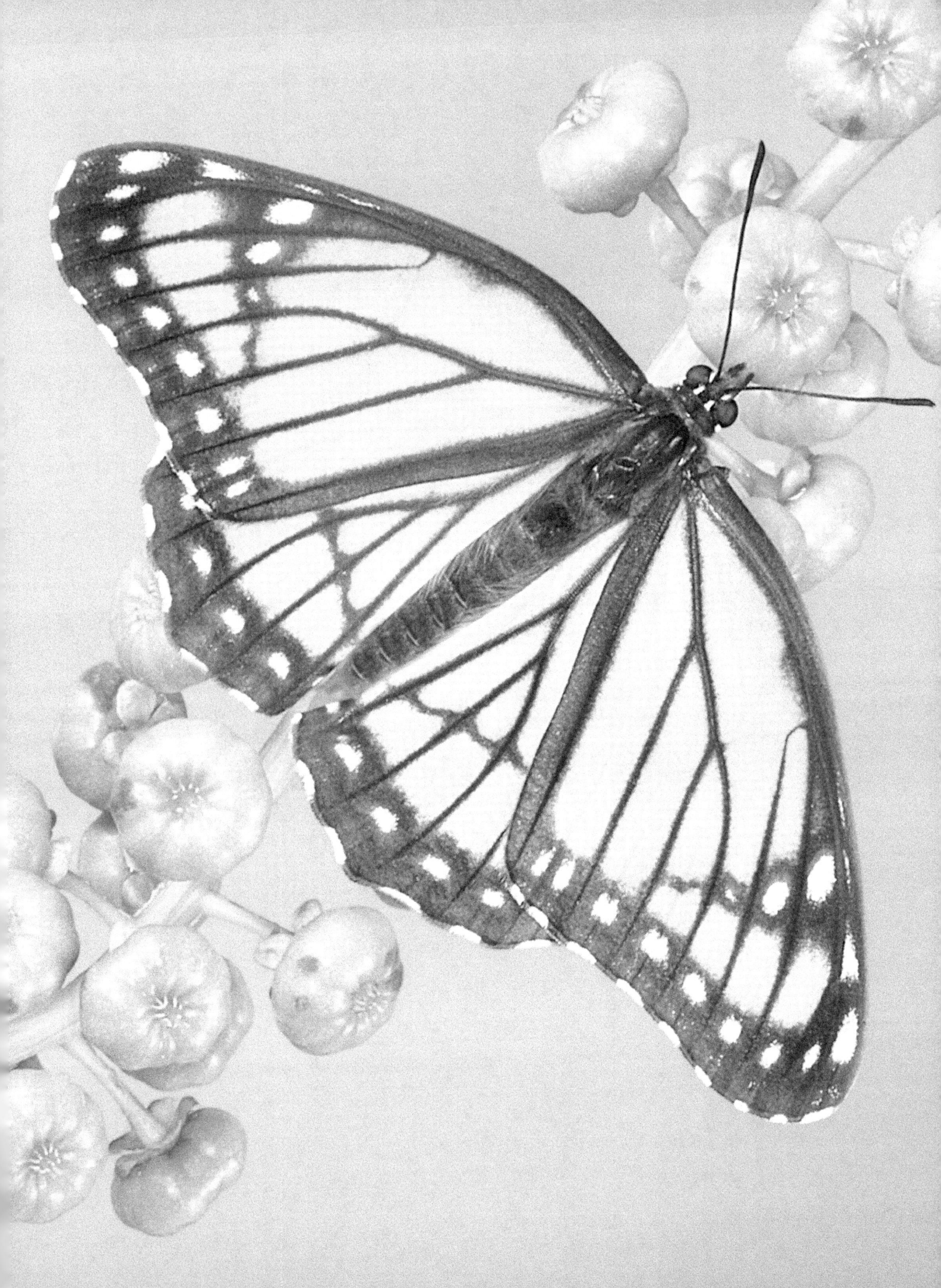

Materials Used:

Colored By:

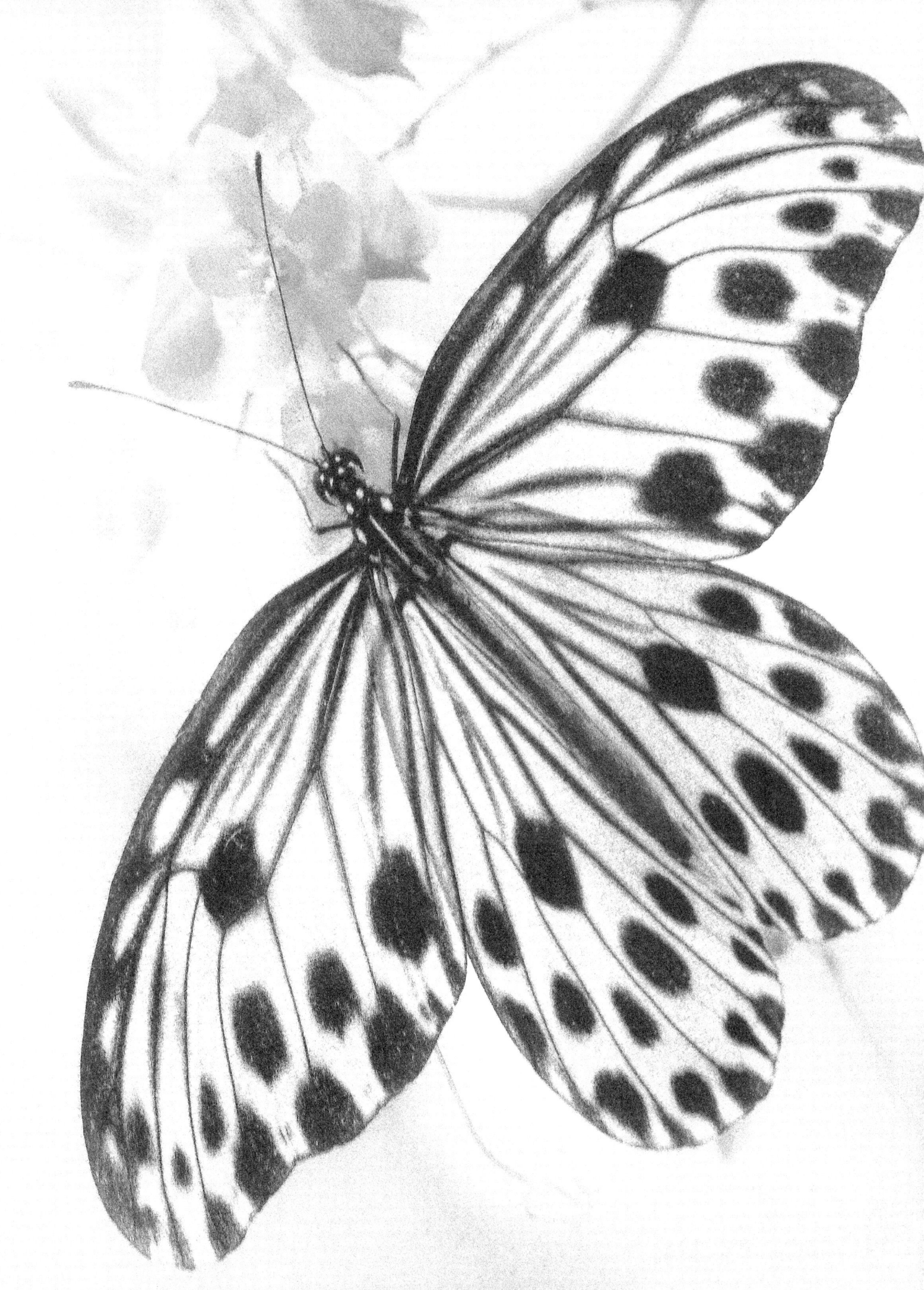